The Sneaky Square

& 113 Other Math Activities for Kids

The Sneaky Square
& 113 Other Math Activities for Kids

Dr. Richard M. Sharp
Dr. Seymour Metzner

TAB BOOKS
Blue Ridge Summit, PA

FIRST EDITION
FIRST PRINTING

Copyright 1990 by **TAB BOOKS**
TAB BOOKS is a division of McGraw-Hill, Inc.

Library of Congress Cataloging-in-Publication Data

Sharp, Richard M.
    The Sneaky square & 113 other math activities for kids / Richard
M. Sharp and Seymour Metzner.
       p.   cm.
    Includes index.
    Summary: Presents math puzzles and enrichment activities within
such topics as speed calculation, logical paradoxes, geometric
puzzles, pattern reasoning, and combinatorial configurations.
    ISBN 0-8306-8474-3   ISBN 0-8306-3474-6 (pbk.)
    1. Mathematical recreations—Juvenile literature.
[1. Mathematical recreations.]   I. Metzner, Seymour, ill.
II. Title.   III. Title: Sneaky square and 113 other math activities
for kids.
QA95.S467 1990
793.7'4—dc20   90-36460
                                                         CIP
                                                         AC

TAB BOOKS offers software for sale. For information and a catalog, please contact TAB Software Department, Blue Ridge Summit, PA 17294-0850.

Questions regarding the content of this book should be addressed to:

    Reader Inquiry Branch
    TAB BOOKS
    Blue Ridge Summit, PA 17294-0214

Acquisitions Editor: Kim Tabor
Book Editor: Susan Lynn Rockwell
Production: Katherine G. Brown
Book Design: Jaclyn J. Boone

Contents

Introduction

................Traps and Conundrums................

................Number Problems................

....................Geometricks....................

....................Combination Puzzles....................

....................Positioning....................

....................Mathematic Relationships....................

..................................Index..................................

Introduction

The Sneaky Square and 113 Other Math Activities is designed to arouse children's interest in mathematical activities, provide practice in basic number operations, and encourage creative approaches to problem solving.

The range of activities appeal to children at many grade levels and of differing abilities and backgrounds. The upper-level math problems should challenge the most apt students while the less difficult activities will intrigue the more reluctant learners. Many motivational learning procedures have been introduced to reinforce the regular classroom mathematics curriculum. These have been proven effective in classroom settings from third to eighth grade.

Directions for all activities are detailed enough so that special training is not necessary for parents or teachers. At the same time, the more advanced students can work independently with the challenges at home or in school. Materials needed are easily acquired; generally paper and pencil or a chalkboard will suffice. Explanations have been provided for each exercise. These explanations provide mathematical perspective without going into unnecessary technical detail.

The 33 activities in Part I: Traps and Conundrums only require basic computational skills with trial-and-error reasoning to reach a solution. These explorations provide a path to a more intuitive understanding of algebra.

The Number Problems, Combination Puzzles, and Mathematic Relationships do not require abstract mathematical reasoning. The problems encourage creative problem-solving that involves number relationships. The Geometricks and Positioning sections include 21 activities that encompass geometric and algebraic principles. They are designed to enable students to develop independent strategies involving these concepts.

Part IV: Logic and Probability involves 30 activities that do not require knowledge of formal logic or probability. Instead, they call for innovative approaches to solving classical problems.

ESP

Difficulty Level: Medium
Materials: Paper, pencils

Tell.............................Show

I will demonstrate that I have a sixth sense. Follow these directions:

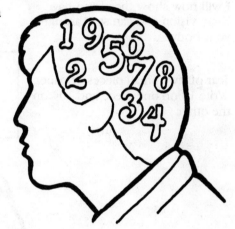

Write any two numbers from 1-9

3, 7

Multiply either number by 5

5×3 = 15

Add 3 to your answer

15 + 3 = 18

36 + 7 = 43

Double the sum you just wrote

When I call on you, tell me your final number and I will tell you your two original numbers.

18×2 = 36

Add to it, the other number you started with

Subtracting 6 will give you a number with the two original digits.
(43 − 6 = 37 = 3, 7)

..........................Explanation..........................

This demonstration depends on algebraic manipulations. Multiplying by 5 and later doubling was really multiplying by 10. Adding 3 became adding 6 with this doubling. In effect, subtracting 6 undid the adding of 6, and separating the answer into individual digits undid the multiplying by 10.

2
X Ray

Difficulty Level: Medium
Materials: None

Tell...........................Show

I will now show the class I have X-ray vision and can see through your body.

Tear off two small pieces of paper. Write 1¢ on one piece and 10¢ on the other.

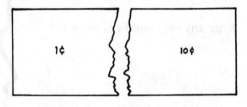

Place a piece in each hand and close your fist. Remember which one is in your left hand and which one is in your right hand.

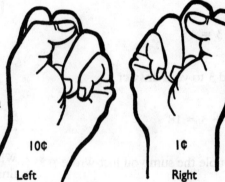

Multiply what's in your right hand by 4. Remember the answer.

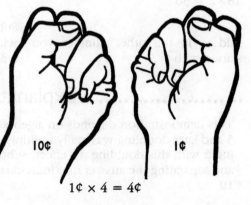

2

Multiply what's in your left hand by 3. (5 or 7 may also be used.) Keep this number in your head.

$$10¢ \qquad 1¢$$
$$3 \times 10¢ = 30¢$$

Add together the two numbers in your head.

$$30¢ + 4¢ = 34¢$$

When I call on you, tell me the answer and I'll tell you which hand has which coin.

If the answer is an even number, the penny is in the right hand. If odd, it's in the left hand.

.... Explanation ....

This trick is based on elementary number theory which says that adding 2 even numbers results in an even number and adding an odd number and an even number produces an odd number. The multiplication with the right hand will always give an even number, whereas the number generated by the left hand will be either even or odd depending on the coin in it.

3
E Pluribus Unum

Difficulty Level: Medium
Materials: Paper, pencils

Tell..........................Show

Write any two numbers from
50–100.

65,83

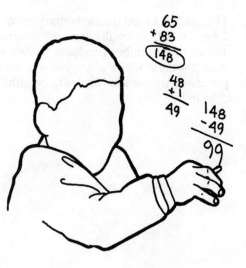

Add them.

Cross out the first digit on the left.

~~1~~48

Add one to the remaining number.

48 + 1 = 49

Subtract this new number from
your original sum. What is your
answer?

148
− 49
———
99

The answer will always be 99

.....................Explanation.....................

This series of steps is related to casting out nines which is inherent in our number system. This is why the sum of the digits in the subtraction is always 18.

4
Ditto

Difficulty Level: High
Materials: Paper, pencils

Tell...........................Show

I will ask one of you to pick your favorite number from 1−9. Write it on the board, work on the board together with the class, and the whole class will give you a present.	7 (Chosen number)

Write the number I am putting on the board. Notice there is no *8* in this number.

1 2 3 4 5 6 7 9

Multiply this number by 7 (or whatever number was chosen by the pupil).

$$\begin{array}{r} 1\,2\,3\,4\,5\,6\,7\,9 \\ \times\,7 \\ \hline 8\,6\,4\,1\,9\,7\,5\,3 \end{array}$$

Multiply your new number by 9. What is your answer?

$$\begin{array}{r} 8\,6\,4\,1\,9\,7\,5\,3 \\ \times\,9 \\ \hline 7\,7\,7\,7\,7\,7\,7\,7 \end{array}$$

.........................Explanation..........................

This is a number oddity in which the sum of the digits in every answer is always a multiple of nine. In this example, multiplying by 7 and then by 9 was, in effect, multiplying by 63, which generated an answer of all 7's, whose sum of digits is 63.

5
Presto

Difficulty Level: Medium
Materials: Paper, pencils

Tell........................Show

I will write a magic number on a
piece of paper, fold it, and ask Carol
to hold it tightly in her hand.

Ann, write a 3-digit number on the board using 3 different digits.	478
Jack, write another 3 digit number right under Ann's.	478 539
Since you have written two numbers, I will also write 2 numbers.	478 539 521 460

Add these four numbers.

478
539
521
460
1998

Carol, read the magic number on
the paper you're holding.   1998

·······················Explanation·······················

The sum is always 1998. Each number the teacher writes must be added
to a pupil's number so that the pair equals 999 as in the diagram:

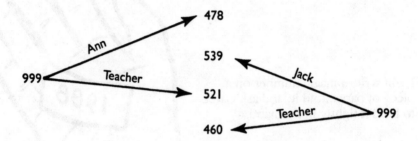

Therefore, you have two 999's or the sum of 1998.

8

6
Speed Demon

Difficulty Level: High
Materials: Paper, pencils

Tell......................Show

I will give you an example of my lightning-fast brain at work. I will ask one of you to write a problem on the board multiplying a two-digit number by another two-digit number.

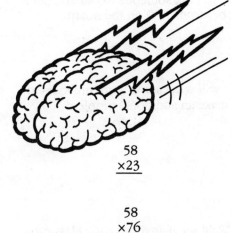

58
×23

I will write a second problem on the board. (The teacher writes the same multiplicand (top number) as the pupil, but the multiplier (bottom number) is the difference between 23 and 99 (99 − 23 = 76).)

58
×76

Teacher note: Your bottom number (multiplier) is found by subtracting the pupil's bottom number from ninety-nine.

The class will now do these two multiplication problems, add together the answers, and see if anyone can get the total before I do it in my head.

Answer: 5742. Subtracting 1 from the top number (58) gives 57, the first 2 digits of the answer, while subtracting the top number (58) from 100 gives the 42, the last 2 digits of the answer.

......................Explanation......................

This shortcut involves the distributive property of multiplication over subtraction and also is linked to casting out nines. In our example, we are multiplying ninety-nine (23 + 76) 58s, but instead, to make things easier, we are multiplying one hundred 58s by simply annexing two zeros to 58 (5800). Because we substituted 100 for 99, we have to subtract a 58 from 5800 (5800−58) which gives the correct answer 5742.

7
Add-Along

Difficulty Level: Medium
Materials: Paper, pencils

Tell......................Show

I will ask someone to put any number from 1–9 on the board.	5

<table>
<tr><td>

I will write some more numbers to make an additional problem.

</td><td>

5 (Every number is 3 more than
8 the preceding number. Any
11 sequence of numbers can be
14 used as long as there is the
17 same amount of increase
20 between them. This challenge
23 works best using an even
<u>26</u> number of terms.

</td></tr>
<tr><td>

We'll see if anyone in the class can add these numbers on his or her paper before I do it in my head.

</td><td>

Answer: 124. In this example the answer is obtained by adding the top and bottom numbers (5 + 26 = 31). Count up the number of terms (8). Take $1/2$ of them ($1/2$ of 8 = 4) and multiply the 4 by the previous sum (4 × 31 = 124).

</td></tr>
</table>

......................Explanation......................

This problem involves an informal method for determining arithmetic sums.

8
Payday

Difficulty Level: Medium
Materials: Paper, pencils

Tell.............................Show

Pretend you are offered an executive position by a billionaire who asks you to choose which one of 2 ways you preferred being paid. You may receive 1¢ the first day, which doubles everyday after that for 31 days a month. For example, the second day you receive 2¢, the third day 4¢, the fourth day 8¢, and so on.

   The other way is to receive $1,000 the first day and an additional thousand dollars every succeeding day. This way you will receive $2,000 the second day, $3,000 the third day, $4,000 the fourth day and so on. Which method of payment would you prefer?

$1,000, $2,000, $3,000, $4,000 etc. after 31 days would amount to nearly a half million dollars ($496,000).

1¢, 2¢, 4¢, 8¢, etc. after 31 days would total more than 20 million dollars!

......................Explanation........................

This situation involves comparing the sum of an arithmetic sequence (1,000; 2,000; 3,000 . . . . .) and the sum of a geometric sequence (1¢, 2¢, 4¢ . . . .). The doubling effect of a geometric sequence gallops along and rapidly overtakes any arithmetic sequence.

9
Card Shark

Difficulty Level: Medium
Materials: Paper, pencils, playing cards (deck)

Tell......................Show

Here's a famous Las Vegas card trick. I will call on volunteers to do simple calculations on the board while I face away from the board.

♣ = 1   ◇ = 2

♡ = 3   ♠ = 4

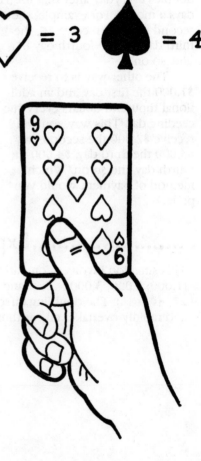

Sue, pick any card from this deck and write both its value and suit on the board. An Ace is one while Jack is 11, Queen is 12, King is 13. Cards 2–9 keep their face value.

Juan, double the value of the card.	$9 \times 2 = 18$
Billie Joe, add 2 to Juan's answer.	$18 + 2 = 20$
Victoria, multiply Billie Joe's answer by 5.	$5 \times 20 = 100$
Hank, look at the suit number chart on the board and add the correct suit number to Victoria's total and tell me your answer.	$100 + 3 = 103$
The card Sue picked is the 9 of hearts.	Subtract ten from the answer ($103 - 10 = 93$) and the left hand digit tells you the card value (9) and the right hand digit is the suit value as shown on the chart (3 = hearts).

...................Explanation.......................

This manipulation involves algebraic reasoning, but is easier to explain in arithmetic terms. Multiplying the card value moves to the ten's place or the hundred's place, and you have an extra 10. Subtracting 10 will undo this. Addition of the suit value (1, 2, 3, or 4) places it in the one's column.

10
Tisket Tasket Basket

Difficulty Level: Low
Materials: None

Tell............................Show

If I had 6 pieces of candy to share among 3 children, how many should each get?

2 candies apiece

A mother baked 9 brownies to share among 9 cub scouts. How could each scout get one but still have one brownie left in the bag?

One scout gets the ninth brownie in the bag

..........................Explanation..........................

The solutions to many problems depend on examining hidden premises.

11
California Express

Difficulty Level: Low
Materials: None

Tell............................Show

The California Express leaves Los Angeles for San Francisco, traveling at 90 mph while at the same time the Pacific Limited leaves San Francisco for Los Angeles, traveling 60 mph. When the trains meet, which one is nearer Los Angeles?

They are equi-distant from Los Angeles.

........................Explanation..........................

Since when they meet they are at the same place, their speed of travel is immaterial, and they are at the same distance from any location.

12
St. Ives

Difficulty Level: Low
Materials: None

Tell..............................Show

As I was going to St. Ives, I met a man with 7 wives. Every wife had 7 sacks. Every sack had 7 cats. Every cat had 7 kits. Kits, cats, sacks, and wives; How many were going to St. Ives?

One

............................Explanation............................

Only the narrator was going to St. Ives because to meet people on the road means they are going in opposite or different directions. This is a traditional puzzle.

13
Bird Brains

Difficulty Level: Low
Materials: None

Tell.......................Show

Jane brought 12 cookies to class. She gave away 4 of them. How many were left?

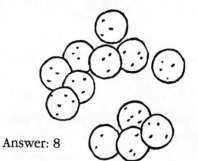

Answer: 8

A farmer saw 11 crows on a fence. He shot 3 of them. How many remained?

Answer: 3

.......................Explanation.......................

Only the dead ones remained, the others flew away.

14
Special Sale

Difficulty Level: Medium
Materials: None

Tell .... Show

A new homeowner bought something that cost:

1 for $1.00
12 for $2.00
144 for $3.00

What item could reasonably account for this pricing?

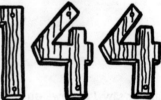

Write "1" on the board.
Write "12" on the board.
Write "144" on the board.

Answer: House numbers

.... Explanation ....

We ordinarily consider numbers as representations of definite quantities. A problem that treats numbers as digits ignoring place value creates distractive ambiguity.

Ambiguity in mathematical language arises when we confuse numbers with symbols. In the above example, we think of 144 as a quantity, of 144 things (number) rather than 3 separate digits or items worth $1 a piece.

15
Midas Touch

Difficulty Level: Medium
Materials: None

Tell.............................Show

Which would you rather have:

4 pounds of $10 silver coins
or
2 pounds of $20 silver coins?

Explain your answer.

Answer: 4 pounds of $10 coins

.........................Explanation.........................

A heavier weight would always be worth more than a lighter weight of the same matter, in this case silver. The worth of each individual coin is irrelevant because worth is dependent on total weight.

16
Tight Fist

Difficulty Level: Low
Materials: Coins

Tell.............................Show

I have 3 coins in my hand. They add up to 45¢. What are the coins?

Answer: 1 quarter, 2 dimes

I now have three coins in my hand. They total 85¢. One is *not* a dime. What are the coins?

Answer: Half dollar, quarter, dime

........................Explanation........................

Saying *one* is not a dime, doesn't mean one of the other two can't be. This is a case of drawing unwarranted inferences from a false premise.

20

17
Dead of Night

Difficulty Level: Medium
Materials: None

Tell.............................Show

A C.I.A. agent's wife told me how her husband died of shock in his sleep. She said he dreamed he was captured and was about to be shot, when a car backfired and the sudden noise killed him immediately. What is wrong with this story?

If the agent died without waking, how could his wife know what he was dreaming?

...........................Explanation...........................

Inferences based on false assumptions lead to erroneous conclusions.

18
What's Cooking

Difficulty Level: Low
Materials: None

Tell.............................Show

A 4 lb., male turkey takes 80 minutes to cook, while a 4 lb., female turkey takes 1 hour and 20 minutes to cook. What might account for the difference in cooking time?

There is no difference.
80 min. = 1 hr. 20 min.

..........................Explanation.........................

Pupils are often distracted by irrelevant information in thought problems.

19
Dating Game

Difficulty Level: Medium
Materials: None

Tell......................Show

A grasshopper on a number line jumps from negative 4 to positive 5. How many jumps did it make?

9 Jumps

-4 -3 -2 -1 0 1 2 3 4 5

A Roman child wrote on his pet's tombstone, "Here lies Fido, born 3 B.C., died 4 A.D." How old was Fido when he died?

3   2   1   1   2   3   4
BC   BC   BC   AD   AD   AD   AD

The real number line has a zero. The calendar number line goes from 1 B.C. to 1 A.D. without a zero, so from 3 B.C. to 4 A.D. is only 6 spaces, or years rather than 7 because there is no zero.

20
Post Office

Difficulty Level: Medium
Materials: None

Tell .... Show

If there are 3 ft. in a yard, how many yards are there in 12 ft.?

$$12 \div 3 = 4$$

If there are 12 one-cent stamps in a dozen, how many three-cent stamps are there in a dozen?

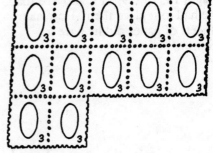

.... Explanation ....

By definition, a dozen of anything contains twelve items.

21
Ink Spots

Difficulty Level: High
Materials: None

Tell.............................Show

A printer made so many errors on pages 14, 15, 79, 115, and 116 that he had to replace them. How many sheets of paper did he have to reprint?

Four sheets

.........................Explanation..........................

All books start with page one on the right hand side. Page 2 would be the other side of page 1. Any pair of consecutive pages starting with an odd number would be one sheet of paper. Any pair of consecutive pages starting with an even number would be two sheets.

22
Hocus Pocus

Difficulty Level: High
Materials: Paper, pencils

Tell.............................Show

Divide 100 by 25 and add 6. What do you get?

$(100 \div 25) + 6 = 10$

Divide 30 by 1/2 and add 10. What is the answer?

$(30 \div 1/2) + 10 = 70$
(Most pupils will answer 25!)

.........................Explanation..........................

When we do division, we are asking how many of the divisors can be taken from the dividend. In this case, we are asking how many 1/2s can be taken from 30, and this would be 60 one-halves.

23
Crime
Doesn't Pay

Difficulty Level: High
Materials: None

Tell.........................Show

A shoplifter in a numismatist's (coin dealer's) store stole the oldest coin he could find, dated 279 B.C. If a rare coin is worth $10 for each year before Christ that it was minted, how much could he sell it for?

Zero dollars

.......................Explanation.......................

The coin had to be counterfeit because the term "B.C." could not have been used then. "B.C." means Before Christ, and the minter could not know Christ was going to be born 279 years after he minted the coin.

24
Neatza Pizza

Difficulty Level: High
Materials: Paper, pencils

Tell............................Show

A party of 8 people ordered a large pizza like the one on the board. The waiter, a real show-off, divided it into 8 equal pieces with only 3 straight cuts of his knife. On your paper, show how he did it.

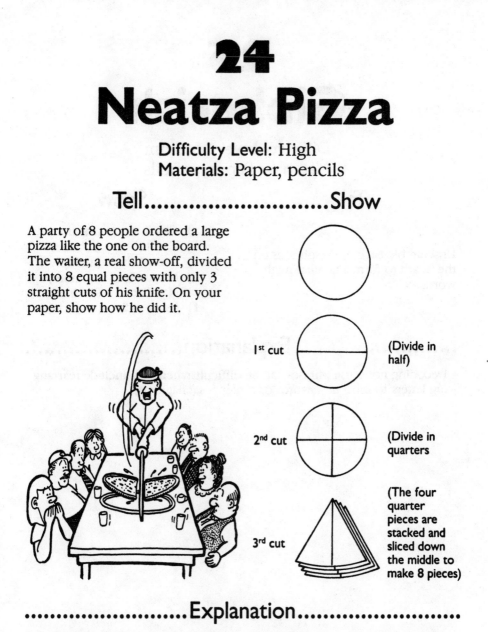

1st cut (Divide in half)

2nd cut (Divide in quarters

3rd cut (The four quarter pieces are stacked and sliced down the middle to make 8 pieces)

..........................Explanation........................

The maximum number of pieces you can make with two cuts is 4. Any third cut in the same plane can make no more than seven pieces. Therefore, a two-dimensional solution doesn't work, and we must look for a third dimension solution, namely stacking the pieces.

25
Gibberish

Difficulty Level: Medium
Materials: Paper, pencils

Tell............................Show

Unscramble each of the phrases on the board to form a familiar math word.

a) Can it for   (fraction)
b) Cart tubs   (subtract)
c) Lumty Lip   (multiply)
d) Me run B   (number)
e) Mad lice   (decimal)
f) I sow vidi   (division)

.........................Explanation.........................

Decoding nonsense phrases can be difficult when they include rearranging letters to form new words or sentences (anagrams).

26
Hazy Dazy

Difficulty Level: Low
Materials: None

Tell.........................Show

The alphabet has 26 letters. How
many are not vowels?

21

Some months have 30 days, some
have 31 days. How many have 28
days?

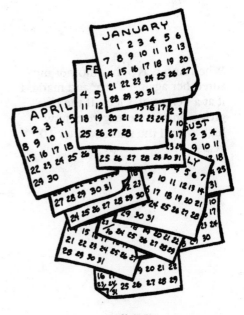

All (12)

..............................Explanation......................

Every month has at least 28 days, although February has only 28 days.
The question did not ask for which month or months had *only* 28 days.

31

27
Tall Tale

Difficulty Level: Low
Materials: None

Tell.............................Show

When Ann was 5, her mother measured her against a tree and marked it at a height of 3 feet. If the tree grows one foot every year, how high would the mark be after 10 years?

3 ft.

........................Explanation........................

A tree grows taller from its top, so the rest of the tree remains at the same height.

28
A Corny Tail

Difficulty Level: Low
Materials: None

Tell..........................Show

Peter Rabbit ate two ears of corn every day for 5 days. How many ears did he eat altogether?

Ten ears

Farmer Jones hid a dozen ears of corn in a box to keep them from Peter Rabbit. But Peter found the box, entered, crawled out with three ears everyday. How long did it take to empty the box?

12 days!

..........................Explanation..........................

Although he left with three ears a day, two of those belonged to him (on his head), so he only took away one ear of *corn* daily.

33

29
Big Dig

Difficulty Level: Medium
Materials: None

Tell........................Show

If 4 men take 6 days to dig a ditch, how long will it take 2 men to dig a ditch half that size?

6 days
Since the men and the job are *both* reduced by half, there is no reason to change the time.

If 2 men can dig a hole in one day, how long will it take 1 man to dig half a hole?

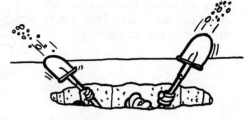

You can't dig *half* a hole.

..........................Explanation........................

Any hole you dig, by definition, is a complete hole. Since a hole can be thought of as zero (nothing), you can't have half of zero or nothing.

30
Cavity

Difficulty Level: Medium
Materials: None

Tell........................Show

How many cubic feet of water can be removed from a Jacuzzi 10 ft. wide, 5 ft. long, and 3 ft. deep?

$10' \times 5' \times 3' = 150$ cubic feet

How much dirt can be removed from a hole that is 3 ft. deep, 2 ft. wide, and 10 ft. long?

None

........................Explanation........................

By definition, a *hole* is a cavity with nothing in it. Therefore, there is nothing to be removed.

31
Topsy-Turvy

Difficulty Level: Low
Materials: Paper, pencils

Tell......................Show

What 3-digit number, turned upside
down, spells a source of energy?

710 = OIL

...................Explanation.....................

Some digits have the configuration of letters when viewed from different perspectives.

32
Tender Trap

Difficulty Level: Medium
Materials: None

Tell.............................Show

I'll say a series of numbers. After each number, the whole class should immediately answer with the next higher number. For example, when I say *fourteen*, the whole class should respond by saying *fifteen*.

Class answers should be put on the board for effect.

Eight	9
Fifty-six	57
Thirty-two	33
One hundred sixty-five	166
Four hundred ninety-nine	500
Four thousand ninety-nine	4,100

Note: The class will almost certainly have been lured into answering *five* thousand. Discuss with them why they made the error.

...........................Explanation.........................

The students are trapped into the mistake of saying *five thousand* because the only place value signal they heard was thousand in *four thousand ninety-nine*.

33
Happy Birthday

Difficulty Level: Low
Materials: None

Tell.......................Show

Dorothy is 5 years old. Tom is 4 years old, and Jose is 8 years old. How many birthdays have all these children had?

$$\begin{array}{r} 5 \\ 4 \\ \underline{8} \end{array}$$

When the children call out the answer "17," the teacher should write down "3" as the answer.

.........................Explanation.........................

A birthday is the day you were born. You may have celebrated it eight times over eight years. but you still had only *one birthday*, namely the day you were actually born.

34
Poison T

Difficulty Level: Medium
Materials: None

Tell...............................Show

On the board are three rows of T's. A class member and I, taking turns, may erase as many T's as we wish from any *one* row. The next player may erase any of the remaining T's on that row or any other row, but again from only one row. The loser is the one who is left with only *one* T to erase, the Poison T.

A) T T T T T
B)   T T T T
C)   T T T

If you force your opponent into any of the following five positions on his or her turn, you will have a definite advantage:

1) T T
      T T

2) T T T
      T T T

3) T T T T
      T T T T

4) T
      T
      T

5) T T T ⎫
      T T ⎬ in any order
      T   ⎭

..........................Explanation.........................

This game is a variation of the ancient game "Nim" which is based on reasoning in binary notation.

35
Candy Store

Difficulty Level: Medium
Materials: Paper, pencils

Tell.............................. Show

Suzy went to the candy store and brought home 100 pieces of candy which cost exactly $1.00. On the board are the three kinds of candy she bought and their prices. How many of each kind did she buy?

10 ¢

5 ¢

2/1¢

Answer:

1 Tootsie Roll	10¢
9 Peppermint Sticks	45¢
90 Jelly Beans	45¢
	$1.00

........................Explanation........................

Inductive thinking together with trial and error experimentation solves this problem.

36
Blockade

Difficulty Level: Medium
Materials: Paper, pencils, marker

Tell................................Show

On the board are 5 numbers. Ann, stand in front of any number you want.

I will now stand in front of another number and the class will add these two numbers together.

Class responds "7"

Ann, please sit down, and Jimmy can stand in front of any of the five numbers except the one I'm blocking. The class will now add this number to the previous total.

Class responds "10"

I will now choose any of the five numbers except Jimmy's, and we will add this number to the last total.

Class responds "11"

We will continue in this manner until either a class member or I stands in front of a number that brings the total to 37. This will be the winner. Anyone who has a total over 37 automatically loses.

Whoever blocks any number that gets the total to 30 can force a "win." All the future moves after 30 are clear except when a pupil blocks "1." The teacher then must block "3" which guarantees a "win."

..........................Explanation..........................

This exercise is an application of the maximum-minimum concept to calculus.

37
Carnival

Difficulty Level: Medium
Materials: Paper, pencils

Tell.............................. Show

A ring toss at a carnival advertises a grand prize for anyone who can total exactly 100 points with 10 tosses or less. More than one ring may be on a number. The numbered stakes are shown on the board.

Answer: Two 16s =   32
         Four 17s =   68
                    ─────
                      100

..........................Explanation..........................

This problem combines addition with inferential thinking to arrive at the unique solution.

38
Lucky Seven

Difficulty Level: Medium
Materials: Paper, pencils

Tell.............................Show

A school custodian had to nail metal numbers on gym lockers. If the lockers were numbered from 1–99, how many 7's would be needed?

20 (7, 17, 27, 37, 47, 57, 67, 70, 71, 72, 73, 74, 75, 76, 77, 78, 79, 87, 97)

[Note that 77 requires *two* 7s.]

..........................Explanation..........................

A correct solution calls for care in visualizing place value.

39
Square Dance

Difficulty Level: Medium
Materials: Paper, pencils, scissors

Tell........................ Show

We will fold our paper into 16 parts.

[Teacher gives appropriate directions.]

Unfold the paper and number the squares as they are shown on the board. Write large. Cut out the sixteen squares.

1	2	3	4
5	6	7	8
9	10	11	12
13	14	15	16

Arrange all these squares with 4 in each row and 4 in each column so each row and each column equals 34. The two diagonals going from corner to corner must also equal 34. An example of one of these is on the board. There are many others. When you make one, raise your hand and if it's correct, you may place your solution on the board. The rest of the class will seek other solutions.

15	6	9	4	= 34
10	3	16	5	= 34
8	13	2	11	= 34
1	12	7	14	= 34

[There are 880 solutions.]

........................Explanation........................

This number sequence is called a 4 by 4 magic square. Any regular number sequence that can be placed in a square (3 × 3, 4 × 4, 5 × 5, etc.) can be arranged into a magic square.

40
Apache

Difficulty Level: Medium
Materials: Paper, pencils

Tell.............................Show

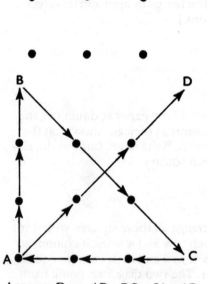

Now each of you should have a partner. On the board I have drawn 9 dots arranged in a square. Draw these on your paper. Taking turns, one drawing and one watching try to connect all dots with 4 straight lines without lifting your pencil from the paper. You must not retrace a line although you may cross over a line. Once you start you must complete the figure or else it becomes your partner's turn.

Answer: Draw AB   BC   CA   AD

....................Explanation........................

The solution depends on not viewing the 9 dots as the boundary of a closed figure thereby forming a mind set that precludes a creative response.

41
Architect

Difficulty Level: High
Materials: Paper, pencils

Tell .... Show

Now each of you should have a partner. On the board I have drawn a house. Taking turns, one drawing and the other watching, try to draw this figure in one continuous line without lifting your pencil off the paper. You must not retrace a line although you may cross over a line. Once you start you must complete the figure or else it becomes your partner's turn.

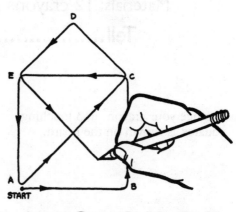

Answer: Draw AB BC CE EA

AC CD DE EB

There are other solutions.

.... Explanation ....

In a topological puzzle similar to the above, you must start at one of the odd vertices and try to end at the other odd vertex. A and B are the odd vertices because they have 3 lines going to them.

42
Slippery Squares

Difficulty Level: High
Materials: 12 crayons per team of 2 pupils

Tell...........................Show

Arrange your crayons in 3 touching squares as shown on the board.

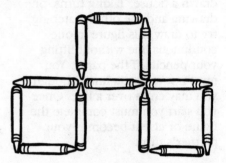

Change the positions of 3 of these crayons so that all the crayons now form 5 squares.

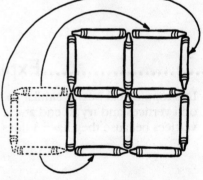

The fifth square is the entire figure which contains the four smaller squares.

......................Explanation........................

The answer depends on having the minimum number of crayons on the perimeter. The most economical area is the one with the smallest perimeter.

43
Triple Threat

Difficulty Level: High
Materials: Paper, pencils

Tell .... Show

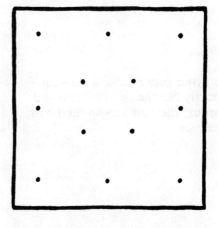

Draw a figure on your paper just like the one on the board.

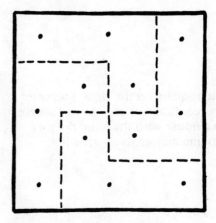

Divide the squares into 4 sections with each section containing 3 dots. The sections must be the same size and shape.

..........................Explanation..........................

The dot distribution calls for the square to be subdivided into congruent six-sided regions. Regular polygonal areas can be partitioned into an infinite number of irregular polygonal regions.

44
Short Circuit

Difficulty Level: High
Materials: Paper, pencils

Tell............................ Show

On your paper, make a drawing
exactly like the one on the board.
Be sure the numbers are in the right
places.

Each square on the right is a power
source. Connect each power source
to a house with the same number.
No line may cross another line.

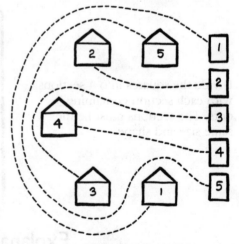

.... Explanation ....

The answer is dependent on the realization that the problem cannot be
solved by simply using straight lines. Topological reasoning separates the
surface interior and exterior regions.

45
Divide and Conquer

Difficulty Level: Medium
Materials: Pencil, paper, straight edge ruler

Tell......................Show

Draw a four-sided figure similar to the drawing on the board.

Answer: 11

Draw 4 straight lines with each line connecting 2 sides of the figure. With these four lines, try to make as many sections as possible inside the figure. Use your straight edge in drawing the lines. The lines may cross each other. You are allowed to try to find a solution as many times as you want.

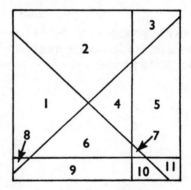

........................Explanation........................

There is a maximum of 11 sections that can be drawn with 4 straight lines. You create the maximum number of sections by having each line intersect all other lines.

46
Sneaky Square

Difficulty Level: High
Materials: Paper, ruler, pencils, scissors

Tell............................. Show

Does everyone have on his or her desk a pair of scissors, paper, a ruler, and a pencil?

On the board you see a rectangle. Its size is 2 inches wide and 10 inches long. Copy this rectangle on your paper. Be sure all four corners make right angles.

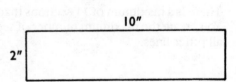

Place your ruler along the top line and put a dot at 4 inches and 8 inches. Do the same with the bottom line and connect the top and bottom dots.

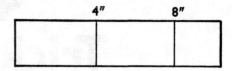

Draw 2 diagonal lines as they are on the board.

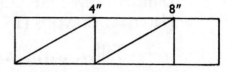

Letter each section as it is on the board.

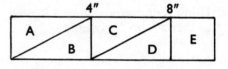

Cut out each lettered section and reassemble them into a perfect square with the letters showing.

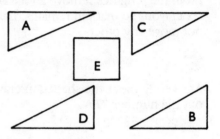

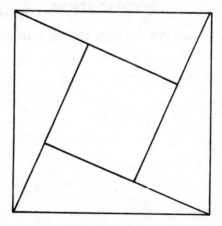

.... Explanation ....

Any rectangle can be transformed into a square. This dissection is a classical Greek approach to visualizing the Pythagorean theorem.

47
Tricky Ten

Difficulty Level: Medium
Materials: Crayons (15 per team of two pupils)

Tell...........................Show

Using your crayons, form 3 figures
as they are on the board.

From the 3 figures remove a total of
six crayons so that ten remains. Do
not move any others.

Answer: Remove the shaded-in crayons and those remaining will spell
out the number *TEN*.

........................Explanation.........................

This manipulation illustrates the need for linguistic precision in express-
ing mathematical ideas.

Fair Share

Difficulty Level: High
Materials: Paper, pencils, ruler

Tell.............................Show

A home builder died and left land to his wife and 4 children. The land was shaped like a perfect square as shown on the board. $1/4$ of the land (Section A) was willed to his wife. The other $3/4$ was divided equally in size and shape among his four children.

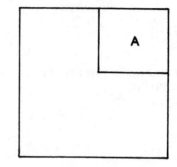

Draw a picture showing how his division was done. Remember each of the four sections must be the same size and shape.

Answer: Divide the original square into fourths. One-fourth (Square A) was already willed to his wife. Since there were 3 squares left to be subdivided among the 4 children, taking one-fourth of the remaining squares gives each son a congruent shape as shown in the diagram below.

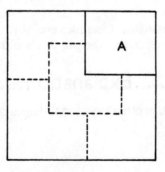

..........................Explanation........................

Area relationships can be interpreted in arithmetic terms and any area can be partitioned into congruent regions.

49
Triangle Trip

Difficulty Level: Medium
Materials: Paper, pencils

Tell.............................Show

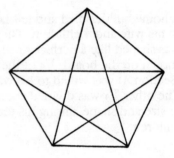

Draw a figure just like the one on the board.

How many triangles can you find in this figure? Some triangles may be part of other triangles.

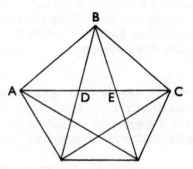

Answer: There are 35 triangles. Examples are ABD, BEC, AEB, BDE, etc. Anywhere there are intersections, the pupils should search for triangles.

.........................Explanation.........................

Polygonal shapes contain other polygonal shapes once the interior chords are drawn.

50
Tennis Menace

Difficulty Level: Medium
Materials: Paper, pencils

Tell.............................Show

Draw a picture just like the one on the board.

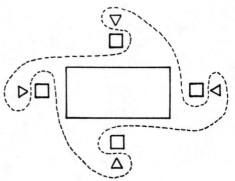

The center figure is a private tennis court. Each triangle and square is a house around the court. All the people in the triangular houses are allowed to use the court because they paid for a membership. The people in the square houses must be kept away from the court because they haven't paid. Draw a fence around the court so that all the people in the triangular houses can get to the court without having to cross the fence but it keeps out the people in the square houses.

........................Explanation........................

Topological surfaces involving continuous paths require an insight into the relationship between interior and exterior spaces.

51
Millennium

Difficulty Level: High
Materials: Paper, pencils

Tell..............................Show

The Denver Dodos, a baseball team, decided they'd like to change their line-up everyday to improve their chances of winning. How long would it take before they had tried every possible line-up arrangement of their 9 players.

Almost 1,000 years!
(994.19 to be exact.)

........................Explanation..........................

This is a permutation problem solved by the following factorial procedure:

$9 \times 8 \times 7 \times 6 \times 5 \times 4 \times 3 \times 2 \times 1 = 362,880$ days or 994.19 years.

$(362,880 \div 365)$.

52
Scramble

Difficulty Level: Medium
Materials: Paper, pencils

Tell..............................Show

Arrange the digits 1–9 in a 3 by 3
square so that no number has a
smaller number following it on the
same row or anywhere below it.
One example of such a square is on
the board. See how many arrange-
ments like this you can make. There
are 42 possible ways.

```
1  3  6
2  5  7
4  8  9
```

...........................Explanation.........................

The top left number must always be one (1) and the bottom right number
must always be nine (9). Once the pupils discern this pattern, other relationships will become apparent. Five possible solutions are:

```
1  4  6      1  2  5      1  3  4      1  2  4      1  3  5
2  5  8      3  4  6      2  6  7      3  5  6      2  4  6
3  7  9      7  8  9      5  8  9      7  8  9      7  8  9
```

53
Gnip Gnop

Difficulty Level: High
Materials: Paper, pencils

Tell..Show

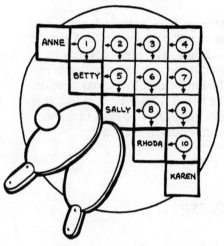

Five girls, Anne, Betty, Sally, Rhoda, and Karen, entered a Ping-Pong tournament. Each girl had to play the others once. In order to do this, how many matches would be played in all.

10 matches

.........................Explanation.........................

In an elementary combinational problem, it is best to analyze the problem by diagramming it as follows:

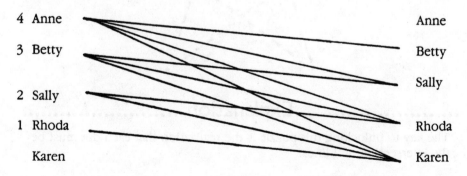

Matches

4 Anne   Anne

3 Betty   Betty

                             Sally

2 Sally

1 Rhoda   Rhoda

Karen   Karen

54
SOS

Difficulty Level: High
Materials: Paper, pencils

Tell........................Show

Arrange 10 dots in such a way that there will be 5 lines with 4 dots in each line. The same dot may be used in two separate lines where the lines cross. In the example on the board, I have 10 dots in 2 lines. You must draw 10 dots in 5 lines, with 4 dots in each line.

Answer:

........................Explanation........................

The key to unlocking this puzzle is the realization that each dot must be the intersection of 2 lines.

62

55
Fill 'er Up

Difficulty Level: High
Materials: Paper, pencils

Tell..............................Show

Make your paper exactly like the diagram on the board. Each box should be large enough to write a number on it.

Using each number from 1–9 only once; fill in the squares so that all four equations are correct.

$$\square - \square = \square$$

$$\square \div \square = \square \quad \times$$

$$\square + \square = \square$$

$$9 - 5 = 4$$

$$6 \div 3 = 2$$

$$1 + 7 = 8$$

..........................Explanation.........................

The clue to solving this set of equations is to complete the multiplication and addition equations.

56
Gypsy

Difficulty Level: Medium
Materials: None

Tell.............................. Show

On the board I have put four magical crystal balls with numbers inside them.

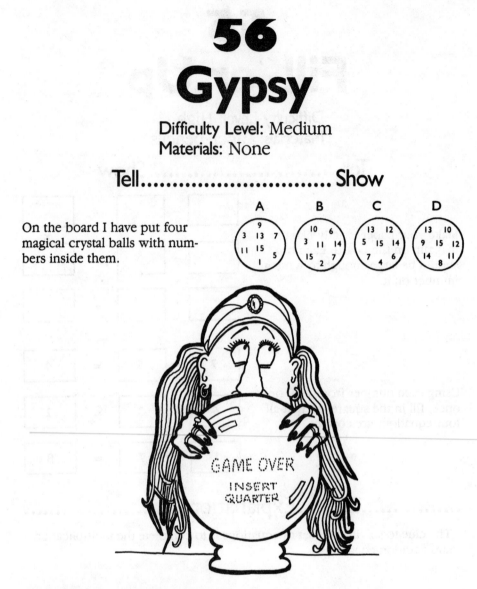

While my back is turned, I will ask one of you to choose a number from 1−15 and put it on the board so the class can see it.

9

Erase the letter above each crystal ball that has this number inside it.

Now erase the number you wrote on the board.

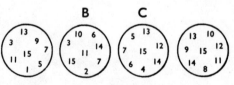

Answer: 9

I will now face the crystal balls and tell you the number you originally chose.

The sum of the bottom numbers in the circles whose letters were erased is always the answer. In this case letters A and D were erased and their bottom numbers were 1 + 8 = 9.

......................Explanation......................

The numbers are placed in the circles according to binary notation. The target (bottom) numbers (1,2,4,8) are all powers of two and all the other numbers in that circle belong to the same power of two.

57
Las Vegas

Difficulty Level: Medium
Materials: 3 dice

Tell...........................Show

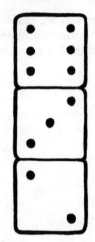

While my back is turned to the board, I will ask one of you to come to the desk, roll the 3 dice and then stack them one on top of another as shown on the board. The pupil stacking them will then write on the board the number of dots on the bottom face marked A, and the two touching faces of B, and the two touching faces of C. The 3 dice shall be returned to the same place in the stack. All 5 numbers should be added together on the board. After this, erase all the numbers on the board. I will turn around, look at the stacked dice with my magic eye, and tell you the secret sum you placed on the board.

You always find the answer by subtracting the top face of the stack from 21. For example, if the top face was 4 dots, then 4 from 21 would give you 17, the secret sum.

........................Explanation........................

Opposite faces of a die always equal 7. With 3 stacked dice, there are 3 pair of opposite faces so 3 sevens equal 21. When you see the top face, subtract this visible part of the 21 which gives you the secret sum.

58
Wizard

Difficulty Level: Medium
Materials: Paper, pencils

Tell................................ Show

I will show you that I am a genuine mind reader. I'll call one of you to work at the board while I face the back of the room and the rest of the class should watch closely to see that all directions have been followed correctly. Do the following:

Write any 3 digit number on the board, using 3 different digits.	186
Using the same digits, switch them around in any way to make another 3 digit number.	861
Line up the larger number over the smaller number.	861 186
Subtract the bottom number from the top number.	861 −186 ——— 675
Erase everything except the answer.	675
Erase one of the digits in the answer and replace it with a box.	6 ☐ 5

6 | 7 | 5

I will now write the missing digit in the mystery box.

Add the digits that can be seen (6 + 5 = 11) and subtract this sum from the next multiple of nine (18 in this case) giving you the missing digit (7).

Teacher note: If the seen digit or digits add exactly to a multiple of nine, the erased digit is nine (9).

.......................Explanation.......................

This demonstration depends on the characteristic of our numeration system and is a reversal of casting out nines.

59
Chain Gang

Difficulty Level: Medium
Materials: Paper, pencils

Tell.............................Show

On the board is an equation with operational signs missing. In each square place either a plus or minus sign so the equation will equal one.

□ □ □ □ □ □ □ □

1□ 2□ 3□ 4□ 5□ 6□ 7□ 8□ 9=1
+ + + − + + − −

There are other solutions.

.........................Explanation.........................

The sum of the numbers 1 through 9 equals 45. The ability to group numbers together to get a difference of one helps solve this equation.

60
Ship Shape

Difficulty Level: Medium
Materials: Paper, pencils

Tell..........................Show

Draw a figure like the one on the board. Using every one of the digits from 4–9, place each one in a circle so that every side equals 21.

Draw a figure like the one on the board. Using every one of the digits from 1–11, place each one in a circle so that every straight line of 3 circles totals 18. The center circle is always used.

Draw a figure like the one on the board. Using every one of the digits from 1–12, place each in a circle so that each straight row of 4 circles adds up to 26.

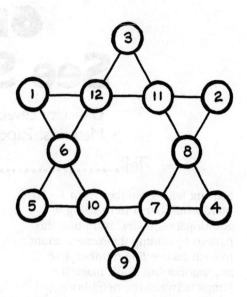

.........................Explanation.........................

Pupils must be able to discover overlapping number relationships to solve these patterns.

71

61
See Saw

Difficulty Level: Medium
Materials: Paper, pencils

Tell.............................. Show

Starting with a number from 1–10, build a number pattern using 8 additional numbers. You build this pattern by adding the same amount to each succeeding number. Use any amount but don't make the jumps between the neighboring numbers too large. A sample is on the board.

2, 5, 8, 11, 14, 17, 20, 23, 26

(each number jumps by 3)

Make a 3 × 3 square like the one on the board.

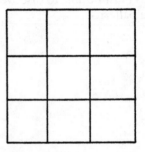

Fill it in with your numbers. The first 3 in the top squares, the next 3 in the middle squares, and the last 3 in the bottom squares.

2	5	8
11	14	17
20	23	26

Add all the numbers together and write their sum on your paper.

126

I will call on one of you to put your square on the board and then we'll see if anyone in the class who hasn't used the same number pattern can get the answer by using paper and pencil before I do it in my head.

The answer will always be 9 times the center square. In the example above, 9 × 14 (the center square) = 126.

......................Explanation........................

In any sequence or number pattern with an odd number of entries, the middle one divides the whole sequence into two parts so that the sum is found by multiplying the middle number (which is the average) by nine because there are 9 entries. Likewise in a sequence with 5 entries, you would multiply the middle entry by 5 to get the sum of the sequence.

62
Bow Wow

Difficulty Level: Medium
Materials: Paper, pencils

Tell..........................Show

In a pet shop, ten dogs wore different tags from 1–10. Two dogs
apiece were placed in each of 5
kennels marked East, West, North,
South, and Central Kennels. In each
kennel, the numbers on the two
dogs are added together. The total
results are shown on the board.
What pair of dogs were in each of
the kennels? There are several solutions.

North Kennel   = 12
East Kennel   = 11
South Kennel   = 8
West Kennel   = 15
Central Kennel = 9

North	= 12	10,2	8,4	9,3	10,2	9,3
East	= 11	7,4	2,9	10,1	8,3	8,4
South	= 8	5,3	7,1	6,2	7,1	6,2
West	= 15	9,6	10,5	8,7	9,6	10,5
Central	= 9	1,8	6,3	4,5	5,4	1,8

The pupils may find other solutions.

..................Explanation..................

This problem primarily uses the skills of renaming sums along with
deductive reasoning.

Stop the Clock

Difficulty Level: Medium
Materials: Paper, pencils, and rulers

Tell.............................. Show

On the board you see the face of a clock. Draw a clock face on your paper and try to make two straight lines across it, so that the clock numbers in each section add up to the same sum.

Each section equals 26.

$$11 + 12 + 1 + 2 = 26$$
$$10 + 9 + 3 + 4 = 26$$
$$8 + 7 + 6 + 5 = 26$$

........................Explanation.........................

The sum of the clock numbers is 78. Two intersecting lines always make 4 sections. Since 78 cannot be divided evenly into 4 sections, we must seek another solution, therefore the lines must not intersect and the clock face must be divided into 3 sections.

64
Oddits

Difficulty Level: Medium
Materials: Paper, pencils

Tell..............................Show

There are 11 ways of adding 8 odd numbers together to make 20. Numbers may be repeated. See how many of these you can get. An example labeled "A" is on the board.

A. $13+1+1+1+1+1+1+1$
B. $11+3+1+1+1+1+1+1$
C. $9+5+1+1+1+1+1+1$
D. $9+3+3+1+1+1+1+1$
E. $7+7+1+1+1+1+1+1$
F. $7+5+3+1+1+1+1+1$
G. $7+3+3+3+1+1+1+1$
H. $5+5+5+1+1+1+1+1$
I. $5+5+3+3+1+1+1+1$
J. $5+3+3+3+3+1+1+1$
K. $3+3+3+3+3+3+1+1$

..........................Explanation........................

These equations may be solved once the pupils understand that 2 odd numbers must equal an even number and they can group numbers appropriately.

65
Sparkle

Difficulty Level: High
Materials: Paper, pencils

Tell.............................Show

Three miners found diamonds weighing 5, 13, 12, 4, 9, 8, 15, 10, and 6 ounces apiece. They each found 3. Tom's diamond weighed twice as much as Dick's. Which three diamonds did Harry find?

5, 13, 12, 4, 9, 8, 15, 10, 6

Answer:

Tom: 8, 10, 12 = 30
Dick: 4, 5, 6 = 15
Harry: 9, 13, 15 = 37

...........................Explanation...........................

Although an algebraic equation could be used, most children will find the answer by using a trial and error procedure.

66
Castaway

Difficulty Level: High
Materials: Paper, pencils

Tell............................ Show

Smokin' Sam was castaway on a desert island with just one box of 64 cigars. He wanted them to last as long as possible and found that by smoking exactly 3/4 of each cigar, he could stick the 4 butts together to make another whole cigar. How many extra cigars can he smoke by using this method?

21 extra cigars

.........................Explanation........................

Sixty-four (64) original cigars make 64 one-quarters (1/4s). Each 4 of those one-quarters (1/4s) makes another cigar which amounts to 16 new cigars. There will be 16 one-quarters (1/4s) left from these. Each of the one-quarters (1/4s) make another whole cigar which amounts to 4 new cigars. The same process repeated with those 4 cigars gives us one new cigar. The total new cigars would then be 21 (16 + 4 + 1).

67
Assembly Line

Difficulty Level: High
Materials: Paper, pencils

Tell..............................Show

$1 + (2 \times 3) + 4 + 5 + (67) + 8 + 9 = 100$

$123 + 4 - 5 + 67 - 89 = 100$

There are many ways of combining every one of the digits from $1-9$ so that they equal 100. These digits, $1-9$, must be arranged in order, and individual digits may be used together to form a number. Create as many similar equations as you can. Two examples are on the board.

Some other solutions:

$1 + 2 + 3 + 4 + 5 + 6 + 7 + (8 \times 9) = 100$

$(1 \times 2) + 34 + 56 + 7 - 8 + 9 = 100$

$12 + 3 - 4 + 5 + 67 + 8 + 9 = 100$

$123 - 45 - 67 + 89 = 100$

$1 + 2 + 3 - 4 + 5 + 6 + 78 + 9 = 100$

........................Explanation........................

Success here depends upon the manipulation of numerical relationships.

Quatro

Difficulty Level: High
Materials: Paper, pencils

Tell......................Show

I will give you a target number from 0−20. You are to reach this number by writing an equation with just 4s. You can only use four 4s in your equation. You may use any operation (+, −, ×, ÷), decimals, and/or parentheses. If the target number was 3, an equation to reach 3 might be (4 + 4 + 4) ÷ 4. I will write this example on the board.

$$(4 + 4 + 4) \div 4 = 3$$

Answers:

$$0 = 44 - 44$$
$$1 = (4 \div 4) \times (4 \div 4)$$
$$2 = (4 \div 4) + (4 \div 4)$$
$$3 = (4 + 4 + 4) \div 4$$
$$4 = 4 \times (4-4) + 4$$
$$5 = [(4 \times 4) + 4] \div 4$$
$$6 = 4 + [(4 + 4) \div 4]$$
$$7 = (4 + 4) - (4 \div 4)$$
$$8 = 4 + 4 + 4 - 4$$
$$9 = (4 + 4) + (4 \div 4)$$
$$10 = (44 - 4) \div 4$$

$$11 = (4 \div 4) + (4 \div .4)$$
$$12 = (44 + 4) \div 4$$
$$13 = 4 + [(4 - .4) \div .4]$$
$$14 = 4 \times (4 - .4) - .4$$
$$15 = (4 \times 4) - (4 \div 4)$$
$$16 = 4 + 4 + 4 + 4$$
$$17 = (4 \times 4) + (4 \div .4)$$
$$18 = 4 + 4 + (4 \div 4)$$
$$19 = [(4 + 4) - .4] \div .4$$
$$20 = 4 \times [4 + (4 \div 4)]$$

Other equations are possible.

......................Explanation......................

Success hinges upon a knowledge of the correct order of operations and seeing interrelationship among numbers.

69
Space Station

Difficulty Level: High
Materials: Paper, pencils

Tell.............................Show

The figure on the board depicts a space station with square landing pads. Number the landing pads so that each straight line of 3 connected pads adds up to 9. The numbers you can use are $2^1/_4$, $1^1/_2$, 0, 3, $5^1/_4$, 6, $4^3/_4$, $3^3/_4$, $3/_4$.

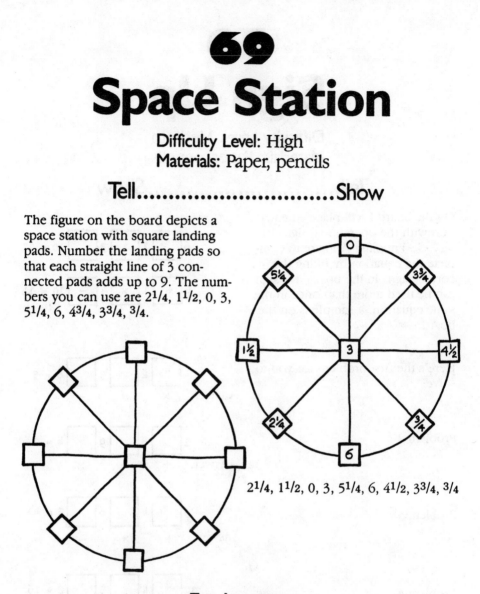

$2^1/_4$, $1^1/_2$, 0, 3, $5^1/_4$, 6, $4^1/_2$, $3^3/_4$, $3/_4$

...........................Explanation...........................

The set of 9 numbers makes a sequence ($3/_4$ difference between numbers) which can be placed in a 3 × 3 magic square.

70
Sign Up

Difficulty Level: Medium
Materials: Paper, pencils

Tell.............................Show

On the board I will place an equation with the operational signs (×, +, ÷, −) missing. You are to complete the equation by filling the correct signs in the boxes. No sign can be used more than once in the same equation. A sample is on the board.

6 □ 1 □ 3 □ 10 = 11

6 + 1 × 3 − 10 = 11

Here's the first problem for you to solve:

4 □ 2 □ 3 □ 6 = 5

Answer: × + −

Problem 2

1 □ 8 □ 9 □ 4 = 0

Answer: + − ×

Problem 3

3 □ 4 □ 6 □ 2 = 40

Answer: + × −

Problem 4

12 □ 4 □ 5 □ 2 = 16

Answer: ÷ + ×

Problem 5

5 □ 7 □ 7 □ 7 = 4

Answer: × − ÷

.........................Explanation.........................

Although trial and error solutions are most common, some pupils may have an intuitive grasp of the mathematical relationships.

71
Checkout

Difficulty Level: Medium
Materials: Paper, pencils

Tell............................ Show

Mrs. Jackson left the supermarket with exactly $1.19 in coins in her purse, with the largest coin a half-dollar. She found to her amazement, in spite of having all these coins, she still couldn't make correct change for a dollar, a half-dollar, a quarter, a dime, or even a nickel. What coins were in her purse?

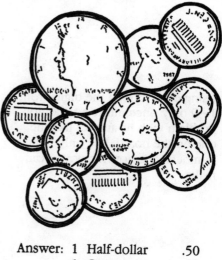

Answer:		
1	Half-dollar	.50
1	Quarter	.25
4	Dimes	.40
4	Pennies	.04
		$1.19

.... Explanation ....

This money problem involves logical thinking due to the restrictions imposed on making correct change.

72
Triple Threat

Difficulty Level: Medium
Materials: Paper, pencils

Tell.............................Show

$$
\begin{array}{r}
738 \\
+ 216 \\
\hline
954
\end{array}
$$

Using every one of the digits from 1–9 only once, make an addition problem with its answer like the one on the board. Use only 3 digit numbers. See how many you can make.

Some other solutions are:

$$
\begin{array}{r}
658 \\
314 \\
\hline
972
\end{array}
\qquad
\begin{array}{r}
564 \\
219 \\
\hline
783
\end{array}
$$

$$
\begin{array}{r}
478 \\
215 \\
\hline
693
\end{array}
\qquad
\begin{array}{r}
192 \\
384 \\
\hline
576
\end{array}
$$

$$
\begin{array}{r}
273 \\
546 \\
\hline
819
\end{array}
\qquad
\begin{array}{r}
259 \\
614 \\
\hline
873
\end{array}
$$

.......................Explanation........................

The digital sum of the answer is always 18 (in the example on the board $9 + 5 + 4 = 18$). Working backwards from this sum, it is easier to generate the addends.

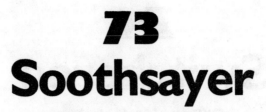

73
Soothsayer

Difficulty Level: Medium
Materials: Paper, pencils

Tell...................................Show

Write 5 consecutive numbers starting with any number from 1–100. An example is on the board.

14, 15, 16, 17, 18

Find the total of your 5 numbers.

80

I will ask you for your total and will tell you the sequence of numbers you chose.

Divide the total by 5 which will give you the middle number of the sequence. Going back 2 numbers from it gives you the first number of the 5 number sequence.

......................Explanation......................

In any sequence with an odd number of entries, the middle one divides the whole sequence into two parts and is the average. Dividing the sum by the number of entries always gives you this average. If the sequence had been 3 entries instead 5, you would have divided by 3 to get the middle number (average).

74
Switcheroo

Difficulty Level: Medium
Materials: None

Tell.............................Show

Top Row:

On the board are two rows of glasses. Half are filled with chocolate milk. By moving only one glass in the top row, make that top row exactly like the bottom row? How can this be done?

Bottom Row:

Answer: Pour the #5 glass into the # 2 glass and return it to its original position.

.......................Explanation........................

A deadlock develops when you try an inflexible interpretation of the problem. Therefore, a creative element, i.e., pouring, must be introduced into the solution.

75
Multi-Jet

Difficulty Level: High
Materials: Paper, pencils

Tell .... Show

I will ask you to get $2/3$ of $3/4$ of certain numbers. One way to do it would be to first find $3/4$ of the number and then find $2/3$ of that answer. For instance, if I give the number 12, you would first find that $3/4$ of 12 is 9, and then $2/3$ of 9 is 6. Now find $2/3$ of $3/4$ of 16. Find $2/3$ of $3/4$ of 24. I will ask one of you to give a number between 1 and 100 which is also a multiple of 4 for all of us to work on using the same procedure. First find $3/4$ of the number and then find $2/3$ of the answer. You will try to get the answer before I write it on a piece of paper and put it in my pocket.

$3/4$ of 12 = 9, and
$2/3$ of 9 = 6.

$3/4$ of 16 = 12, and
$2/3$ of 12 = 8.

$3/4$ of 24 = 18, and
$2/3$ of 18 = 12.

The answer will *always* be $1/2$ of the given number!

.... Explanation ....

Three-quarters of any number on can be shown as follows:

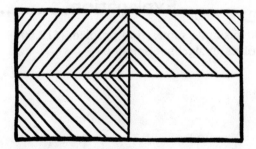

Three-quarters of this figure refers to the shaded parts and it can be seen that two of these shaded parts is one-half of the original square or number. The mathematical equation for this is:

$$2/3 \times 3/4 = 6/12 = 1/2$$

76
Fun and Games

Difficulty Level: High
Materials: Paper, pencils

Tell......................... Show

Sharon went to a game store and
bought a chess set and a book
which together cost $12.50. The
chess set cost $2.50 more than the
book. How much did each cost?

Chess set	$ 7.50
Book	$ 5.00
	$12.50

.... Explanation ....

This seems like a simple subtraction problem ($12.50 − $2.50 = ?) but
actually it involves an algebraic solution.

77
Computique

Difficulty Level: Medium
Materials: Paper, pencils

Tell........................... Show

I will call on a pupil to give me my two-place number and I will multiply it by eleven in my computer brain and get the answer before anyone in the class can figure it out.

The digits of any two-place numbers are the outside numbers in the answer. The middle number in the answer is found by adding these two digits. So, with 45, the outside numbers in the answer are 4 and 5 and the middle is the sum of 4 and 5 (9). Therefore, 45 × 11 = 495. However, when the 2 digits add up to more than nine carry a one to the first outside number. With 75 × 11, 7 + 5 = 12, so the one is added to the 7 and the answer is 825.

.........................Explanation.........................

This is a shortcut method involving place value manipulation.

78
Squaresville

Difficulty Level: Medium
Materials: Paper, pencils

Tell .... Show

I will call on a pupil to give me any two-place number ending in a 5, and I will multiply it by itself (square it) and get the answer mentally before anyone in the class can do it on paper.

Take the first digit of the number and multiply by the next higher digit and then place "25" at the end of that answer. For example, with 65 × 65, take the 6 and multiply it by 7 (42) and place 25 after it (4225).

.... Explanation ....

This is a shortcut method involving the place value manipulation.

Omni-Fun

Difficulty Level: High
Materials: Paper, pencils

Tell.............................Show

Using every one of the digits from
1–9 once, make up a multiplication
problem with its answer. A sample
problem is on the board.

$$\begin{array}{r} 297 \\ \times\ 18 \\ \hline 5346 \end{array}$$

Some other solutions:

$$159 \times 48 = 7632$$
$$157 \times 28 = 4396$$
$$198 \times 27 = 5346$$

.........................Explanation........................

Trial and error will provide solutions.

Full House

Difficulty Level: Medium
Materials: Paper, pencils

Tell...................................Show

Using every one of the digits 1−5
once, devise a multiplication equation (problem and answer).

$13 \times 4 = 52$

....................Explanation....................

The basic requirement to complete this is to have a knowledge of the multiplication table.

81
Robin Hood

Difficulty Level: Medium
Materials: Paper, pencils

Tell..............................Show

You are Robin Hood, and I will ask you to shoot a particular score using the fewest possible arrows. For example, a score of 7 would have to hit the 4, 2, and 1 rings with 3 arrows.

(A) shoot a 25
(B) shoot a 19
(C) shoot a 47

Answer:

(A) 16, 8, 1
(B) 16, 2, 1
(C) 32, 8, 4, 2, 1

..........................Explanation........................

Any whole number up to 63 can be formed on this target. Each number is a power of 2 which allows any whole number to be written which is one less than the next succeeding power. On this target, the next succeeding power would be 64.

82
Ultra

Difficulty Level: Medium
Materials: Paper, pencils

Tell........................... Show

Using all the digits from 1–5 once, make a multiplication problem which provides the largest possible answer.

$$\begin{array}{r} 431 \\ \times\ \ 52 \\ \hline 22{,}412 \end{array}$$

........................Explanation........................

Pupils must understand that larger numbers must be used in the higher place value positions.

83
Caboose

Difficulty Level: High
Materials: Paper, pencils

Tell......................Show

I will call on a pupil to write a 3-digit number on the board. The class will try to beat me in figuring out a digit to attach at the end of this number in order to make the whole 4-digit number exactly divisible by 9.

Add the individual digits of the 3-digit number and subtract this total from the next multiple of nine. This subtraction answer is the number you need to attach to the end of the given 3 digit number.

Sample: 471 = 4 + 7 + 1 = 12.

Eighteen is the next multiple of nine and 12 from 18 leaves 6. Attaching the 6 to the end of 471 makes it 4716 which is now divisible by 9 (4716 ÷ 9 = 524). If adding all digits comes to an exact multiple of 9, you may attach either "0" or "9" to the 3-digit number.

..........................Explanation..........................

Adding individual digits is the standard divisibility test for nine.

84
Hide n' Seek

Difficulty Level: High
Materials: Paper, pencils

Tell.............................Show

There is an addition problem on the board with an incorrect answer. You can make this answer correct by removing certain digits in the problem.

```
 111
 333
 555
 777
 999
1111
```

On your paper, show how the addition problem should look in order to get this answer.

```
 111
   3
   7
  99
1111
```

..........................Explanation..........................

This exercise depends on knowledge of our numeration system and the ability to see combinations that equal eleven.

85
Candy Cutter

Difficulty Level: Low
Materials: None

Tell.................................Show

Tim cut his licorice stick into 12 equal pieces and took 5 seconds to make each cut. If he started cutting at 3:17 p.m., when would he finish?

3:17:55 (55 seconds after 3:17)

..........................Explanation..........................

It takes only 11 cuts to make 12 equal pieces as shown in this diagram:

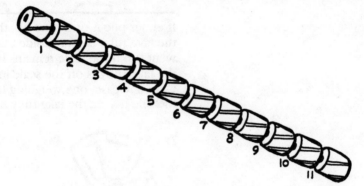

86
Ruby Roundup

Difficulty Level: Medium
Materials: Paper, pencils

Tell.............................Show

A jeweler bought 9 rubies and learned that one of them was a fake that would weigh less than the real ones. How could he find the fake ruby with only 2 weighings of the rubies on his balance scale?

1)

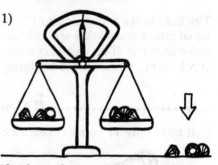

If either pile A or B goes up, then the fake ruby is on the side that went up. If the scale remains level, the fake ruby is off the scale in pile C. In any case, one weighing locates the pile having the fake ruby.

2)

Take the pile which has the fake ruby and arrange it as shown above. The side that goes up has the fake ruby or if the scale stays level the ruby off the scale is fake.

............................Explanation............................

The ability to use inferential thinking in a sequential fashion leads to the correct conclusion.

87
7-11

Difficulty Level: High
Materials: Paper, pencils

Tell.............................Show

A Chinese cook has to boil rice for exactly 15 minutes, using a 7-minute hourglass and an 11-minute hourglass. How can he do this? Illustrate your solution.

Start both hourglasses together with the rice off the fire.

When all sand in the 7-minute hourglass is on the bottom, place the rice on the fire. There will still be 4 minutes of sand left in the top of the 11-minute hourglass.

When these 4 minutes have passed, all the sand will be on the bottom of both hourglasses and the rice has been boiling for 4 minutes. Turn the 11-minute timer over, it will start again and this 11 minutes plus the previous 4 will total 15 minutes boiling time.

.........................Explanation.........................

This exercise is an adaptation of a famous problem involving creatively arranging known elements into a new configuration.

88
Weigh Out

Difficulty Level: High
Materials: Paper, pencils

Tell...............................Show

Farmer Jones uses a balance scale to weigh any produce from 1 – 40 lbs. He needed only 4 weights which he used in various combinations. These weights were 1, 3, 9, and 27 lbs., which could be placed on either side of the scale. Illustrate how he would weigh out the following amounts of produce:

(A) 12 lbs.
(B) 37 lbs.
(C) 25 lbs.
(D) 32 lbs.
(E) 20 lbs.

(A)

(B)

(C)

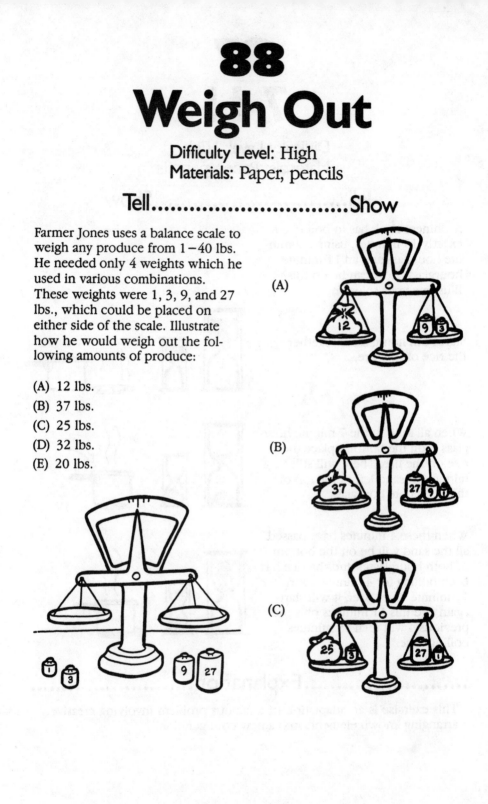

(D)

(E)

.... Explanation ....

This is a form of Bachet weight puzzle based on the ternary (base 3) numeration system.

89
Ship Ahoy

Difficulty Level: Medium
Materials: None

Tell..Show

A ship at anchor has a rope ladder 12 feet long hanging from it. The rungs on the ladder are 1½ ft. apart with the first rung touching the water. If the tide rises at 6 inches per hour, how long would it be before the first 5 rungs are under water?

They will never be under water because the ship rises with the tide along with the attached ladder.

......................Explanation......................

This solution is an application of the buoyancy principle and the numerical information is irrelevant.

90
Alphabet Soup

Difficulty Level: Medium
Materials: None

Tell......................Show

On the board is a picture of two bowls of alphabet soup. The letters in each bowl belong together because they share a certain characteristic in common. Place each of the letters S, T, U, and V in the correct bowl and be ready to give a good reason for choosing that bowl.

Answer: T, and V should be grouped with A, E, F, and H. S, and U belong with B, C, D, and G.

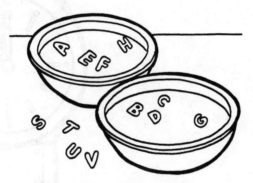

......................Explanation......................

The letters in the top bowl can all be formed with straight line strokes while the others require curved strokes. This problem involves categorical thinking based on perceptual cues.

91
Scaley Tale

Difficulty Level: High
Materials: None

Tell.............................Show

If 5 fishermen catch 5 fish in 5 minutes, how long would it take 50 fishermen to catch 50 fish?

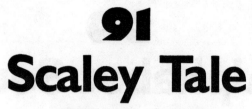

5 minutes

..........................Explanation.........................

You must assume it takes each fisherman 5 minutes to catch a single fish. Therefore, the time element would never change regardless of how many fishermen and fish are involved. This is an example of axiomatic reasoning.

92
Razzle Dazzle

Difficulty Level: Medium
Materials: None

Tell...........................Show

A quarterback's brother died and left all his money to his only brother. However, the quarterback never received any of this money even though it was legally paid out. How could this happen?

The quarterback was a girl!

...........................Explanation...........................

Difficulties in figuring out the answer are related to stereotyped linking between sexes and "appropriate" jobs leading to a false assumption i.e., quarterbacks *must* be men.

93
Lunch Bunch

Difficulty Level: Low
Materials: None

Tell...............................Show

The principal asked a teacher how many kids were still in the lunch line. The teacher replied, "There is one kid in front of 2 kids, a kid behind 2 kids, and a kid between 2 kids." How many kids were in the lunch line?

Answer: 3 kids

....................Explanation....................

This demonstrates order relationships and shows 3 different ways of describing each position (kid).

94
Gumball

Difficulty Level: Medium
Materials: None

Tell......................Show

Jack and Jill went up the hill to get gumballs from a penny machine. The machine had 30 red gumballs and 30 green gumballs. If they got 1 gumball for each penny they put in the machine, how many pennies would they spend before they could be certain of sharing two gumballs of the same color.

Answer: 3 pennies

........................Explanation........................

After the second penny, you would have either: (a) 2 gumballs of the same color or (b) two gumballs of different colors. A third penny would deliver a gumball that had to match one of the colors.

95
Bye-Bye Birdie

Difficulty Level: Low
Materials: None

Tell............................Show

Dolly and Dotty were playing badminton in their backyard when the birdie fell into a hole. It was so deep they couldn't reach it by hand or with any stick. How did they finally get the birdie back?

Answer: They flooded the hole with water, and the birdie floated to the top.

..........................Explanation..........................

Flexible thinking and a knowledge of the physical principle of buoyancy solves this problem.

96
Arabian Nights

Difficulty Level: High
Materials: 3 black markers,
3 white markers, 3 boxes

Tell.........................Show

When Ali Baba was traveling in Arabia, he was faced with this problem. The Sultan showed him 3 boxes which had 2 pearls apiece concealed in them. He was told that one box contained 2 white pearls (WW), one had 2 black pearls (BB), and the third box had a black and a white pearl (BW). The boxes were marked BB, WW, and BW but each box was marked incorrectly. The Sultan ordered Ali-Baba to label the boxes correctly, allowing him to take only *one* pearl from *any* box he wished. If he succeeded, he would keep the 6 pearls, but if he failed, his head would be chopped off. You are to figure out the only sure way for him to solve his problem and be prepared to explain it.

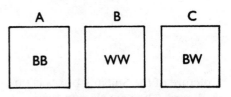

Ali Baba must choose a pearl from the box marked BW which must be mislabeled. If he takes out a black pearl, then the other pearl must also be black because the only other choice would be WW which is impossible since he drew a black.

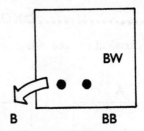

On the other hand, if he draws a white, then there must be a WW in Box C.

109

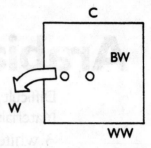

If white were drawn, we know that this box should be labeled WW. Let's assume it's the white pearl that was drawn and therefore the box should be labeled WW.

A picture of the Sultan's boxes is on the board. They are also on my desk.

By taking the WW label from Box B to its correct placement on Box C, we leave Box B with no label. Since we know Box A is mislabeled, its label belongs to Box B because it's the only place for it. This leaves the BW label for Box A. The correct labels are as follows:

·····················Explanation·····················

This is a classical case of using deductive reasoning to solve a logic situation.

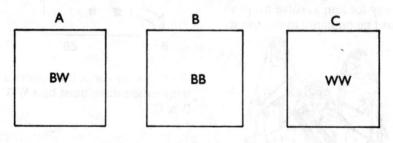

97
Antricks

Difficulty Level: Medium
Materials: None

Tell..............................Show

An ant, starting from the 12-inch end, crawls along the edge of a ruler. It covers half the distance in 12 seconds. How much longer would it take the ant to reach the 1-inch mark?

10 seconds

..........................Explanation..........................

The diagram below shows there are 6 intervals from the 12-inch to the 6-inch mark, and since the ant averages 2 seconds per interval, it takes a total of 12 seconds to cover the distance. However, from the 6-inch to the 1-inch mark there are only 5 intervals, and at the same speed it would take 10 seconds to cover this distance.

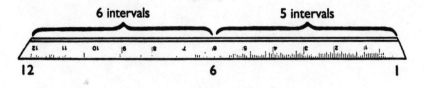

6 intervals   5 intervals

12   6   1

98
Big Ben

Difficulty Level: High
Materials: Paper, pencils

Tell.............................Show

Big Ben, London's largest clock, signals the time with loud bongs. If it takes 3 seconds to make 3 bongs at 3 o'clock, how many seconds will it take to make 6 bongs at six o'clock?

7¹/2 seconds

.........................Explanation.........................

The "bonging" for 3 o'clock may be shown as follows:

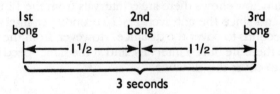

The first bong accounts for the interval from 1 to 2, the second bong accounts for the interval from 2 to 3 which ends with the third bong. Therefore, the 3 seconds have to be divided in half since there are only two intervals for the 3 bongs, averaging $1\frac{1}{2}$ seconds per interval.

At six o'clock, there are 5 intervals totaling $7\frac{1}{2}$ seconds as shown below:

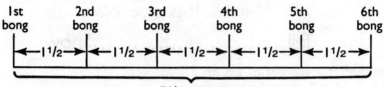

99
Fuelish

Difficulty Level: High
Materials: Paper, pencils

Tell.............................Show

A motorcyclist ran out of gas on a small road off the highway and needed exactly 2 gallons for his tank. A helpful trucker had 2 empty cans holding 5 gallons and 8 gallons, respectively. How could the biker use these cans to measure out the needed 2 gallons? Illustrate your answer.

Answer:

First fill the 5 gallon can and empty it into the 8 gallon can. Then refill the 5 gallon can and pour as much as you can (3 gallons) into the 8 gallon can, leaving the needed 2 gallons in the 5 gallon can.

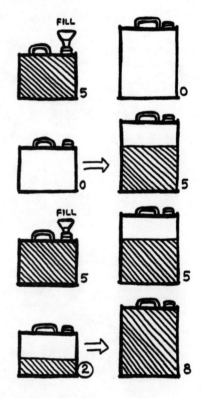

........................Explanation........................

This is a time-honored decanting problem based on divisibility analysis.

100
Wall Ball

Difficulty Level: Medium
Materials: None

Tell.............................Show

There are 24 players entered in a racquetball singles tournament in which each match loser is eliminated. How many matches must be played to determine who wins the cup for first place?

23 matches

........................Explanation..........................

Each time a match is played, one player is eliminated. After 23 matches are played, only the winner remains. Diagrammatically it can be shown as follows:

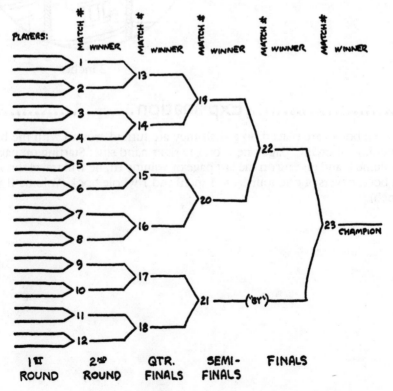

101
Bookworm

Difficulty Level: High
Materials: Paper, pencils

Tell............................Show

A hungry bookworm is eating its way through an encyclopedia set on a library bookshelf. Each book cover is $1/4$ inch thick while the pages are 1 inch thick. If the bookworm starts on page 1 of Volume I and eats its way on a straight path to the last page of Volume III, how far will it have traveled?

2 inches

........................Explanation........................

When books are placed on a shelf they are turned around with the back bindings showing, page one is on the right hand side. Starting on page 1 Volume I, and ending on the last page of Volume III, he will travel through 4 book covers (4 one-fourths = 1 inch) and 1 whole book (Volume II = 1 inch).

102
Link Think

Difficulty Level: Medium
Materials: Paper, pencils

Tell............................Show

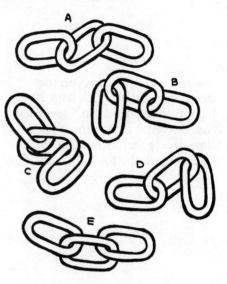

Andy has 5 sections of chain he can link together to make a bike chain. Each section has 3 links as shown on the board. If it cost 5¢ to cut open a link and 10¢ to weld it shut, what is the least amount of money it would cost to join the five sections?

Answer: 45¢

...........................Explanation...........................

Instead of cutting all the end links, cut *each* link in Section E so you will have 3 open links. One of these links will join Sections A and B, the second link joins Sections B and C, while the third link joins Sections C and D, and weld all three links. This makes 3 cuts (15¢) and three weldings (30¢).

103
Day Crawler

Difficulty Level: Medium
Materials: None

Tell...........................Show

A worm trying to climb up the steep, slippery wall of a dam 20 ft. high, manages to climb 5 feet each day. However, during the night it slips back 4 feet. How long will it take to reach the top?

16 days

......................Explanation......................

The worm makes a net gain of 1 foot for each 24 hour day. After 15 days it will be 5 feet short of the top of the 20-foot high dam. The 5-foot move during the 16th day puts it over the top.

104
Jaws

Difficulty Level: Medium
Materials: None

Tell............................Show

A stranger in an isolated village had a throbbing toothache and had to decide which of the town's two dentists should take care of it. He saw that one dentist had a beautiful modern office with new equipment, and this dentist's teeth showed visible evidence of excellent dental work. The other dentist had a plain office with old fashioned equipment, and his teeth showed the effects of poor dental work. Which dentist should the stranger choose and why?

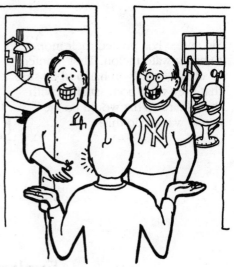

The stranger should choose the dentist who had the plain office and poor teeth.

........................Explanation........................

This logic situation is a version of Russell's Paradox. Dentists cannot work on their own teeth, therefore each showed the effects of the other one's work because there are only two dentists in town.

105
Watermelon

Difficulty Level: Low
Materials: None

Tell.............................Show

Sid and Sylvia pooled their money to buy a watermelon. They wanted to slice it exactly in half and be sure that they were both satisfied with their share. What would be the fairest way to do this?

The fairest way is to have one person cut the melon while the other gets first choice.

......................Explanation........................

According to the Bible, a similar dilemma was solved by King Solomon.

106
Reunion

Difficulty Level: High
Materials: None

Tell.............................Show

At a class reunion, Mr. Blue, Mr. Gray, and Mr. White sat together. The man with the blue shirt said, "Have any of you noticed that although the colors of our shirts are the same as our names, none of us is wearing a shirt that is the same color as his own name?" "Yes, you're right," answered Mr. White. What color shirt was each man wearing?

Mr. Gray—blue shirt
Mr. White—gray shirt
Mr. Blue—white shirt

........................Explanation........................

Since each man's name cannot match the color of his shirt, the man with the blue shirt who was talking must be Mr. Gray or Mr. White. However, Mr. White answered him so the only name remaining for the blue-shirted man is Mr. Gray. Mr. White cannot be wearing the white shirt and since the blue shirt is being worn by Mr. Gray, this leaves the gray shirt for Mr. White. The remaining match has to be Mr. Blue with the white shirt. This logic riddle requires syllogistic reasoning.

107
Sandwich

Difficulty Level: Medium
Materials: None

Tell........................Show

What arithmetic symbol can we place between 20 and 5 to give an answer larger than 4 but smaller than 25?

Solution:

$$20 \quad 5 =$$
$$20 - 5 = 15$$

What arithmetic symbol can we place between 8 and 9 to give an answer larger than 8 but smaller than 9?

Solution:

$$8 \quad 9 =$$
$$8 \bullet 9 = 8.9$$

....................Explanation....................

It can quickly be seen that the operational symbols $(+, -, \times, \div)$ do not solve the problem and some other symbol is needed.

108
Down Under

Difficulty Level: High
Materials: Paper, pencils

Tell .... Show

A sheep rancher in Australia gets
1¹/2 lbs. of wool from 1¹/2 sheep in
1¹/2 days. How many lbs. of wool
will he get from 6 sheep in 7 days?

28 lbs. of wool

...........................Explanation.........................

Since he gets 1¹/2 lbs. from 1¹/2 sheep in 1¹/2 days, doubling the sheep
would double the amount of wool in the same period of time, i.e., 3
lbs. from 3 sheep in 1¹/2 days (Row B in chart below). Reducing the
time to one day is cutting the time by ²/3 (1 day is ²/3 of 1¹/2) and
would reduce production by ²/3, giving 2 lbs. of wool, i.e., ²/3 of 3 lbs.
= 2 (Row C). Doubling the number of sheep would double the wool
production in the same amount of time (Row D). Multiplying the number of days by 7 would also multiply the wool production by 7, giving
28 lbs. (Row E).

	Sheep	Wool	Days
A	1¹/2	1¹/2	1¹/2
B	3	3	1¹/2
C	3	2	1
D	6	4	1
E	6	28	7

109
Boutique

Difficulty Level: Medium
Materials: None

Tell..Show

Two mothers and two daughters went shopping together. Each bought a dress for $50.00. How much did they spend altogether?

$150.

........................Explanation........................

Only 3 dresses were bought, since the women who went shopping were 3 members of the same family, consisting of a grandmother, mother, and daughter. The following diagram shows how this order relationship can be seen as 2 mothers and 2 daughters:

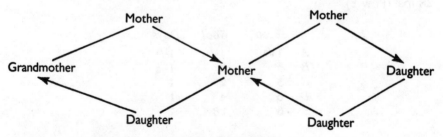

This is an example of equivalence relationship.

124

110
Chic Chick

Difficulty Level: Medium
Materials: None

Tell............................Show

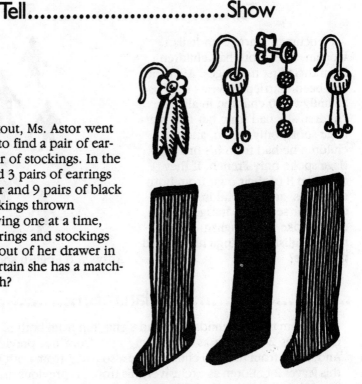

During a blackout, Ms. Astor went to her drawer to find a pair of earrings and a pair of stockings. In the drawer she had 3 pairs of earrings mixed together and 9 pairs of black or brown stockings thrown together. Drawing one at a time, how many earrings and stockings must she take out of her drawer in order to be certain she has a matching pair of each?

Answer: 4 earrings and 3 stockings

..........................Explanation........................

She could draw 3 different times without having a matched pair of earrings. The fourth pick would guarantee an earring to match one of the previous three.

She could draw 2 times without having 2 matching pairs of stockings. The third pick would insure a stocking to match one of the other two.

III
United Nations

Difficulty Level: High
Materials: Paper, pencils

Tell.............................Show

A Frenchman married an Italian woman. They both had children from their first marriages. After they had been married 12 years they had a family of 10 children in all. The children she had from her first marriage spoke only Italian, and the children he had from his first marriage spoke only French. If they each had 8 of their own from both marriages, and the children born after their second marriage to each other spoke only English, how many English speaking children did they have?

Answer: 6 English speaking children

..........................Explanation..........................

Since from their 10 children he had 8 children from both of his marriages, this leaves 2 children as exclusively hers from her previous marriages. And, since from their 10 children she also had 8 from both her marriages, this leaves 2 children as exclusively his from his previous marriage. Therefore, already having 4 children between them when they got married, they had to get another six children to bring the total to 10. These six spoke English. This might be illustrated with a Venn diagram as follows:

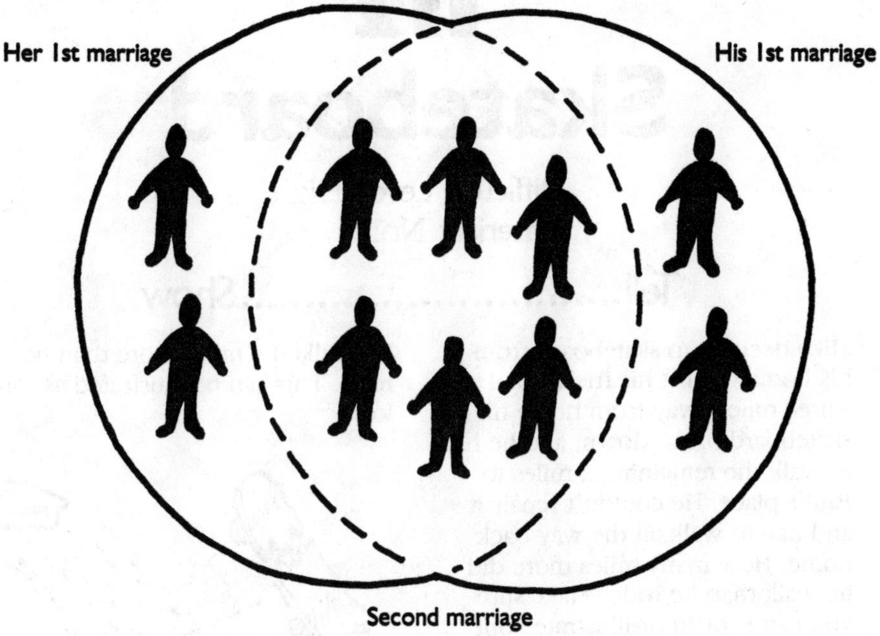

Her 1st marriage

His 1st marriage

Second marriage

112
Skateboard

Difficulty Level: High
Materials: None

Tell......................Show

Mike decided to skateboard from his home to visit his friend Paul. Three miles away from home his skateboard broke down, and he had to walk the remaining 2 miles to Paul's place. He couldn't repair it and had to walk all the way back home. How many miles more did he walk than he rode? Make sure you can explain or illustrate your answer.

He walked 4 miles more than he rode. This can be illustrated as follows:

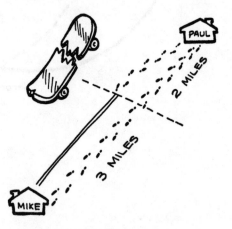

It can be shown that between his home and the breakdown point, he walked and rode the same distance (3 miles). From the breakdown point to Paul's home he had to walk both ways which totals the extra 4 miles.

......................Explanation......................

This verbal problem involves analytical thinking more than computational skills. A sophisticated analysis could render an algebraic solution.

113
Shake, Rattle & Roll

Difficulty Level: High
Materials: None

Tell........................... Show

A gambler bought 7 large boxes of dice with each die weighing exactly 10 grams. However, a friend tipped him off that one of the boxes had dice in which each die in the box was lighter by 1 gram. With just one weighing, how could he determine the lighter box? The seven boxes are shown on the board.

Take one die from Box #1, take two from Box #2, take 3 from Box #3 and continue until you have taken 7 from Box #7. Weigh these dice together, and they should weigh 280 grams.

129

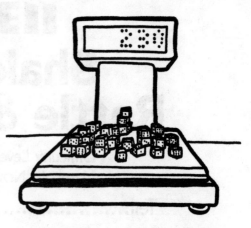

If, for example, Box #5, contained the lighter dice, the total would not be 280 but 275 since 5 lighter dice came from that box. The same reasoning would hold true for any of the boxes.

Solving this puzzle is dependent upon using the principles of deductive reasoning.

114
Crisscross

Difficulty Level: High
Materials: Paper, pencils

Tell........................Show

A farmer going on a trip with a squirrel, acorns, and a fox had to cross a river in a boat in which he couldn't take more than one of them with him each time he crossed. Since he often had to leave two of them together on one side of the river or the other, how could he plan the crossings so that nothing gets eaten, and they all get across the river safely? Try to illustrate your crossings.

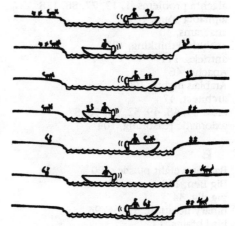

........................Explanation........................

To solve this problem, you must realize that the fox won't eat the acorns, but will eat the squirrel. The farmer has to carry one of the three with him in the canoe to avoid this problem.

Index